Healing is in the Atonement

The Power of the Lord's Supper

RANDY CLARK

Apostolic Network of Global Awakening
1451 Clark Street
Mechanicsburg, PA 17055

For more information on how to order this book or any of the other materials that Global Awakening offers, please contact the Global Awakening Bookstore.

ISBN: 978-1-937467-35-7

globalawakening
1451 Clark Street
Mechanicsburg, PA 17055
www.globalawakening.com
1-866-AWAKENING

Global Awakening
{ Core Message Series }

It is our desire to bring the messages of the Kingdom to the people of God. We have taken what we consider to be core messages from Randy Clark's sermons and schools and printed some of them in booklet form. We hope this teaching increases your understanding of God's purposes for the times we are in and that you find yourself encouraged in your faith. Other core messages are available and they are listed at the end of this booklet.

Table of Contents

Healing is in the Atonement

I'm going to touch on some of the highlights and ramifications of Is Healing in the Atonement? Basically, there are different views about healing. Some say healing is not in the atonement. Others say it is through the atonement but not in the atonement. Then still others say that healing is in the atonement in exactly the same way that forgiveness of sin is in the atonement. I would like to share that based upon the best Old Testament language studies and commentaries from linguists like Michael Brown, the language teaches that healing is in the atonement in the same way that forgiveness is in the atonement. These teachings are based on the original Hebrew language. People who do not believe healing is in the atonement have never really based their beliefs on what the actual text says. Instead, their beliefs are based upon pastoral problems that are associated with teaching that healing is in the atonement. They struggle to understand that if that argument is valid, why isn't everyone healed who believes for their healing? Having said that, I will say that I understand that there is a problem. I understand that it's a pastoral issue. But the text still stands as to what the word says. The death of Jesus on the cross provides the basis for our faith and healing.

Sentimental Prayer

Have you ever heard anyone pray like this? You're praying for someone, let's say it's someone who has been in the church for years, and they've been loved by everybody. Maybe they're cousins to everybody. The prayer goes something like this: "Oh, Lord. Please heal Uncle John. Please heal him because You know he helped build this church. He's been faithful. He's served as a trustee for 42 years. Lord, he was on the session (or whatever your governing board is called). And, Lord, I'm asking you to heal him because you know that he's a good man. He's been a good man; he's been a good father. So, Lord, I'm asking you to touch and heal Uncle John."

Have you heard those kinds of prayers? That is sentimentalism. As I think about it, I know that God understands. However, in some ways it is almost an affront to His character. That kind of prayer implies this: "Lord, I know you are forgetful so I want to remind you about Uncle John because you may not remember." As if we need to remind God about what Uncle John has done.

Secondly, this type of praying is basing our faith on the premise that God would be moved because of what Uncle John did, not on the basis of what Jesus Christ, His Son, did on the cross. It is putting the work of Uncle John in the place of Jesus' work on the cross. It is very common. It is also very natural to pray this way, especially when it is a loved one we are praying for. I believe it is part of human nature.

But sentimental prayers do not move God. Faith moves God. It is as if we are offering up to God the work of the person being prayed over. There is not one scriptural verse that says anything about a promise based upon our works. That is not what is going to move God to heal. But there are

4

many promises about God being moved to heal based upon the new covenant and what Jesus did on the cross.

This is one type of prayer that we often pray for the sick. But don't do that! God is not forgetful. He knows everyone and everything we have done. We don't have to remind Him of anything. Sometimes it sounds like we are trying to convince God to change His mind and to be gracious. Yet the glory of God revealed to Moses when He passed by was the revelation of His goodness, His graciousness. If need is what moves God, there would be more miracles in India than anywhere, because the need there is so great. But need is not what moves God. Sentiment is not what moves God. The works that we may have done are not what move God. What moves God is faith in the work that Jesus did on the cross and the new covenant that God made with us as a result.

Petitionary Prayer

Now, a second way that I hear people praying sometimes, that is also unhealthy and has very little fruit in it, is the petitionary prayer. That is when we are petitioning God to heal. Then we end the petitionary prayer with, "If it's Your will." I have heard people pray that way often. First, you cannot find anyone (Jesus, Paul, Peter, Phillip, Steven) in the Bible that prayed for a person to be healed in that manner. That prayer model does not exist in the New Testament with regards to praying for a person's healing. Scripture does talk about asking the Father "in My name" in petitionary prayers for things other than healing.

However, most of the prayers of the New Testament with regard to healing, prayers that came from Jesus, Peter and Paul, were prayers of command. They commanded something to change through the authority of Jesus' name. Remember, we are seated with Christ in heavenly places, and we have been delegated the authority. When we understand that authority, we understand the prayer of command. We are not commanding God when we pray prayers of command. We are commanding the situation to change. We are commanding the tumor to disappear. We are commanding the vertebrae to move. We are commanding new myelin sheaths to be formed. We are not commanding God to do it, but we understand that we are co-heirs with Jesus, seated with Him in heavenly places. We know that all things are put under His feet. We have been placed above powers and principalities. From that position of delegated authority, we are using the authority God has given to us to pray prayers of command that can be literally creative in the situation at hand, or to cause things that should not be there to disappear.

To be honest, it is hard to get used to praying that way, especially when our prayers have always been from the perspective of asking God to do everything. A friend of mine who is a pastor told me one day that he was listening to the associate pastor of the church he was attending at the time. The pastor was praying a prayer that was basically asking God to bind the spirits. The whole prayer was about, "God, we ask you... We ask you... We ask you..." As he was listening to the associate pastor pray that way, he heard the Lord in his mind telling him, "I won't do it." That caused him to ask the Lord why, especially since it was the associate pastor who was doing the praying. The Spirit told him that He was not going to do for us what He has asked us to do (for ourselves). He said that He had delegated the authority to the believers to do these things. If He has already given to us the delegated authority to do these things, then why would He turn around and do them for us? If He did them for us, we would not be stepping into the place of growth and partnership with Him that He wants us to be in.

Praying with Confidence

It is important to have a sense of what God's will is to begin with. If we do not sense that something is God's will to heal us in our situation, then we cannot pray the prayer of faith. We will always be in doubt if we are not sure what God's will is. If our theology is weak about God's will pertaining to healing of sickness and disease, then it will be hard to pray the prayer of faith. It is the prayer of faith that raises people up and heals them. It is also difficult to pray with certainty if we doubt God's will.

In I John 5: 14-15:

[14] Now this is the confidence that we have in Him, that if we ask anything according to His will, He hears us. [15] And if we know that He hears us, whatever we ask, we know that we have the petitions that we have asked of Him (NIV).

Now the key is in verse 14. It is important that we try to discern the will of God when it comes to healing. If we are not sure that it is God's will to forgive us for our sins, wouldn't it be more difficult for us to come to the assurance of salvation? There was a time when there was a real debate that you could not know for certain that you were in the elect. In that case, you might ask God to forgive you, but He might not forgive you because you were not really among the elect. If you were not among the elect, then you could not be forgiven.

About two hundred years ago there was great insecurity over the assurance of salvation. The only way you could determine if you really were part of the elect was to try to look back over your life and see if you had been living faithfully, having fruit that would bear witness to the fruit of repentance in your life. Then you could have assurance that you really were among the elect. Many people struggled; they could never get any assurance of their salvation. There was no strong sense at that time that it was God's will, always God's will, to forgive our sin if we confessed it. When there was no place of certainty, people really struggled praying through for healing. They had trouble laying hold of the reality of their conversion.

That was one of the genius factors of early Methodism in Wesley; heart-felt religion that you could know that you have been justified because of the effect of the Spirit in your life. You could feel and know that you had been born again. Regeneration was an experience that you could know that you had entered into. But that premise was fought for hundreds of years. There was not the assurance that it was always God's will to forgive sin if we only confessed it. People had no security. Lacking conviction made if more difficult for them to pray through for healing because they did not know that it was God's will to forgive them of their sins.

In like manner, it is difficult for people to pray with confidence if we are forever creating a theology of healing that leaves the issue of God's will as an uncertainty. We believe now that we can be forgiven because Jesus bore our sins, carried our iniquities at the cross.

Suffering Servant

I would like to take a look at the NIV's traditional rendering of Isaiah 52:13 to Isaiah 53:12. This is the great Suffering Servant passage that captures the essence of the meaning of the cross. This is the way you would see it translated in almost every English translation.

Isaiah 52

¹³ See, my servant will act wisely; he will be raised and lifted up and highly exalted. ¹⁴ Just as there were many who were appalled at him—his appearance was so disfigured beyond that of any man and his form marred beyond human likeness — ¹⁵ so will he sprinkle many nations and kings will shut their mouths because of him. For what they were not told, they will see, and what they have not heard, they will understand.

Isaiah 53

¹Who has believed our message and to whom has the arm of the Lord been revealed? ² He grew up before him like a tender shoot, and like a root out of dry ground. He had no beauty or majesty to attract us to him, nothing in his appearance that we should desire him. ³ He was despised and rejected by men, a man of sorrows, and familiar with suffering. Like one from whom men hide their faces he was despised, and we esteemed him not.⁴ Surely he took up our infirmities and carried our sorrows, yet we considered him stricken by God, smitten by him, and afflicted. ⁵ But he was pierced for our transgressions, he was crushed for our iniquities; the punishment that brought us peace was upon him, and by his wounds we are healed. ⁶ We all, like sheep, have gone astray, each of us has turned to his own way; and the Lord has laid on him the iniquity of us all. ⁷ He was oppressed and afflicted, yet he did not open his mouth; he was led like a lamb to the slaughter, and as a sheep before her shearers is silent, so he did not open his mouth. ⁸ By oppression and judgment he was taken away. And who can speak of his descendants? For he was cut

off from the land of the living; for the transgression of my people he was stricken. ⁹ He was assigned a grave with the wicked, and with the rich in his death, though he had done no violence, nor was any deceit in his mouth. ¹⁰ Yet it was the Lord's will to crush him and cause him to suffer, and though the Lord makes his life a guilt offering, he will see his offspring and prolong his days, and the will of the Lord will prosper in his hand. ¹¹ After the suffering of his soul, he will see the light of life and be satisfied; by his knowledge my righteous servant will justify many, and he will bear their iniquities. ¹² Therefore I will give him a portion among the great, and he will divide the spoils with the strong, because he poured out his life unto death, and was numbered with the transgressors. For he bore the sin of many, and made intercession for the transgressors.

In verse three where it says "sorrows," it is the Hebrew word *makob* which can be translated as "pain."1 It should be pain. And the word for "suffering" is the Hebrew *chalah* which is almost always translated as "sickness" or "disease" and yet here it is translated "suffering." In the natural, almost always that word in Hebrew is translated the other way, but here they did not translate it the way it normally would have been.

Next, look at the word "took up" in verse four. In Hebrew, the word is *nasah*. It means "to lift from, carry away." And the word "infirmities" is again the Hebrew *chalah* which means "sickness and disease." The word "carried" is the Hebrew word *sabal* meaning "to carry, bear the weight of" our sorrows. Again, the word for "sorrows" there is the word *makob* which means "pains."

In verse four, He *nasah* (lifted up, carried away) our sicknesses and diseases, which is translated here as "infirmities" and He *sabal* (carried) our sorrows (or pains).

In verse five "pierced" means "to penetrate the body, injure or kill." The Hebrew word for "transgressions" is *pesha'* (rebellion, defiance and defense).

In verse 11 "and he will bear their iniquities" is again "bear our sicknesses" in the alternate translation.

In verse 12, "For he bore the sin of many," is the word *nasah*. In verses 11 and 12 the verbs are *sabal* and *nasah*, "to lift up or carry away" which are the exact same words that were used in verse 4: "He took up (*nasah*) and He bore our infirmities, carried our sorrows or pains."

"Sorrows" does not sound like disease to me. Does it to you? So when they say Jesus is carrying our sorrows, it could be to bring emotional healing for us. However, in the actual Hebrew it is much stronger than in the English. It was mistranslated in English for so long because scholars thought the language was too strong; connecting it to sickness and disease being dealt with at the cross in the same way that sin/ iniquity was dealt with.

Recently, the Holman translation actually translates it correctly:

⁴ Yet He Himself bore our sicknesses, and He carried our pains;

In Matthew's gospel chapter 8, verse 17 he quotes from Septuagint:

¹⁷ This was to fulfill what was spoken through the prophet Isaiah:

"He took up our infirmities and carried our diseases."

Instead of using the word "pains" he used the word "diseases" which is more accurate. There are many scriptures we could allude to but for now I am going to look at one more. In the New Testament, the Apostle Peter drew upon this passage from 1 Peter 2:24: "He Himself bore our sins in His body on the tree so that we might die to sin and live for righteousness. By His wounds you have been healed." This is in the past tense. When were you healed? You were healed at the cross of Jesus. When were you forgiven? At the cross. Thus, how then do we receive forgiveness? It is already been paid for; it is already been dealt with. Our sin has been handled; it has been carried. It has been paid for at the cross. We need to appropriate it then by faith.

In the exact same way, so were our sicknesses already paid, carried and borne in His body, and by His stripes we are healed. But here in Peter it says "have been healed".

Sickness is not God's Will

Now look at Matthew 8:16 NIV:

16When evening came, many who were demon-possessed were brought to him, and he drove out the spirits with a word and healed all the sick. 17 This was to fulfill what was spoken through the prophet Isaiah: "He took up our infirmities and carried our diseases."

Why is this important? If your view of God is the blueprint world view, then everything that happens to you, God either caused to happen or in His permissive will He allowed it. It is like saying that everything that comes to you is God's will. That's very difficult. If it is His will that I am sick, how can I know if it is His will to heal me? Or, if it's His will that this sickness has come for some better purpose, to disciple me, to make me better, then how can I know if it is His will to heal me? The problem with this kind of thinking comes from the verses that talk about the positive benefits and the rewards of suffering. In the New Testament, in this context, these verses never deal with suffering from physical illness and disease. Rather it is suffering because of our witness on behalf of Christ and the gospel. Basically, these particular verses are about persecution, tribulation. Those things do work good in us. And it is not to say that God can't work good things out of sickness when it comes, but that is a hugely different thing than saying that God willed something to happen to us. If that is what we believe, it becomes almost impossible to pray in faith expecting God to heal us. We would feel like we were asking Him to heal us for something that He gave us. Would that make sense?

As long as we question where sickness comes from we will have trouble praying the prayer of faith. In John 10:10 Jesus said: "The thief comes only to steal and kill and destroy; I have come that they may have life, and have it to the full." It says of Jesus in I John 3:8b that He came to destroy the works of the devil. In Acts 10:38 it says, "How God anointed Jesus of Nazareth with the Holy Spirit and power, and how He went around doing good and healing all who were under the power of the devil, because God was with him." That passage says that Jesus healed all who were under the power of the devil. Based upon Acts 10:38, where does sickness have its origin? It's from the devil. You can't pray the prayer of faith when there is doubt about God's will.

Types of Healing

Now there are different types of healings. There is the type of healing that comes through the prayer of faith in James 5:15; "and the prayer offered in faith will make the sick person well; the Lord will raise him up." We see this type of healing in Mark 11:24 also - that if you pray and believe and do not doubt in your heart, that what you have been asking for will be done for you. There are great promises about the prayer of faith. But I have seen people get healed that didn't have any faith. I have seen people be healed by the gift of healing when the individual was not moving in the gift of faith. They had a gift of healing. These are similar gifts, but they are not the same. I have literally seen people healed by this grace for healing. They were healed by the anointing. They were healed in the gift. But, the person who was praying really couldn't be characterize as a person of great faith.

I do not want to make this overly complicated except to say that if we oversimplify it, then we end up with something like, "Well, I don't feel that I can pray the prayer of faith, therefore is there any hope?" The answer is yes, there is still the operation of just the gift of healing. You might say, "Now wait a minute. I thought everything had to come out of faith." The response is that there is a gift of faith and there is a prayer of faith. And there is an atmosphere of faith. Remember; where there is more faith there is more healing in a place. Nevertheless, I have seen Jesus heal people when the person didn't believe in healing. And they got healed. I've seen Jesus heal people when the people that prayed for them, and they got healed, their response (to the prayers) was to be surprised. They would ask, "Really? Are you sure you're healed? I can't believe that."

Healing in Communion

If healing is in the atonement, the atonement is the way by which we're placed in right-relationship with God through what Jesus did at the cross. The cross is the heart of the new covenant. Healing is in the new covenant. Healing is in the Kingdom. When we ask for the Kingdom to come, and we have some understanding that in the Kingdom there is healing, more will take place. Healing is in the new covenant. That means that healing is in communion.

In I Corinthians 11:20-32:

20 When you come together, it is not the Lord's Supper you eat, 21 for as you eat, each of you goes ahead without waiting for anybody else. One remains hungry, another gets drunk. 22 Don't you have homes to eat and drink in? Or do you despise the church of God and humiliate those who have nothing? What shall I say to you? Shall I praise you for this? Certainly not!

23 For I received from the Lord what I also passed on to you: The Lord Jesus, on the night he was betrayed, took bread, 24 and when he had given thanks, he broke it and said, "This is my body, which is for you; do this in remembrance of me." 25 In the same way, after supper he took the cup, saying, "This cup is the new covenant in my blood; do this, whenever you drink it, in remembrance of me." 26 For whenever you eat this bread and drink this cup, you proclaim the Lord's death until he comes.

27 Therefore, whoever eats the bread or drinks the cup of the Lord in an unworthy manner will be guilty of sinning against the body and blood of the Lord. 28 A man ought to examine himself before he eats of the bread and drinks of the cup. 29 For anyone who eats and drinks without recognizing the body of the Lord eats and drinks judgment on himself. 30 That is why many among you are weak and sick, and a number of you have fallen asleep. 31 But if we judged ourselves, we would not come under judgment. 32 When we are

*judged by the Lord, we are being disciplined so that
we will not be condemned with the world.*

What is this passage saying? In Matthew 26:27 it says,

*²⁷"After supper Jesus blessed the cup and He said,
'This cup is the new covenant in My blood which is
shed for many for the remission of sins'*

The cup represents His blood. Leviticus 7:11 says
"without the shedding of blood there is no remission of
sins." The cup is the part of Jesus' death that handles our
forgiveness of sin. Just like Psalm 103:2 and 3:

*² Praise the LORD, O my soul, and forget not all his
benefits ³ who forgives all your sins and heals all
your diseases.*

Two things are mentioned as benefits of what God has
done for His people. He has forgiven us of all our sins and
healed us of all our diseases. These are the benefits of being
related, being in the new covenant with God; forgiveness
and healing. As we look at the new covenant: "This cup is
the new covenant in My blood which is shed for many for
the remission of sins," (1 Cor 11:25) If the cup is for the
remission of sins, what is the bread for? The bread is for
healing for the body. And by His stripes we are healed. If
we do not discern the body, do we understand all that Jesus
did for us at the cross? Do we understand in the same way
that we understand the blood was shed for the forgiveness of
sin? There is a payment that has been paid by Him with His
body to deal with our sicknesses.

Now, there is another reason why this is extremely
important. As we take communion and we understand and
discern the body, we can believe for healing. And, by the
way, in the history of the church, many people received

healing because they understood this about communion. Nothing focuses us more on grace than the cross.

Wrong Thinking

One of the reasons that some people have trouble receiving healing is that they somehow, in a twisted way have been deceived by the enemy. There is nothing more deceiving than deception. Or, as a friend of mine says, "Deception is very deceiving." The enemy is sly. One of the things that cause some people to have difficulty believing that God would heal them is that they think that sickness is a penalty against them, a payment for their sin. Now if you fully appropriate grace, then that sin has been paid for. I do not have to continue in sickness. But some people, even subconsciously I believe, sense that they deserve to be sick because they have not measured up.

That really was stronger in certain periods of church history where the pastors were trained in school to tell the people, "You are sick because of some sin in your life. God is using this sickness to bring discipline into your life so that you will be perfected and become a better Christian. This sickness is actually working toward your perfection. It is maturing you."

Many Catholics have trouble receiving healing because they have been taught to believe that they are carrying and fulfilling the cross of Jesus in their own bodies. They believe that this is what God is calling them to do.

There is another view that I have seen in the church a lot, in Protestants and Catholics both. It goes this way. I have something wrong with me, but it's not that big. Therefore, I am not going to ask God to heal me of this problem because there are people dying in our church. The logic behind it goes something like this: "Since God doesn't have that much healing power to go around, then let's save it and use it on the really desperate ones." That really is the logical conclusion to that type of thinking.

God has enough healing for the really serious ones and your hangnail too. We need to be grounded in an understanding of grace so that we are not trying to pay the penalty for our sins by staying sick. I have prayed for people that when I start talking to them, I find out that they are thinking this way: "I don't deserve to be healed. I've brought this on myself. I have violated the laws of God. I've not handled my toxic emotions correctly." That may be very true, but let's get forgiven. Let's receive forgiveness from God, forgive ourselves and move forward on the basis of discerning forgiveness of sin and the knowledge that the penalty has been paid for the sickness too. Unforgiveness between you and toward anybody else can hinder your healing. Unforgiveness toward yourself can also hinder your healing. This is one of the things I work on.

Christianity vs. Other Religions

No religion should be as effectual in healing the sick as the Christian religion. Yet, one of the reasons we do not see more healing of the sick in Christianity is that there is a sense of internalized guilt that can be an impediment to healing.

Hinduism, upon which New Age teaching is based, is based in kharma. Just spend some time in India where they believe in kharma. You will see the ramifications. In Hinduism, whatever it is that is happening in your life, that is your kharma. You earned it; you worked for it. That is justice. If you do not improve, then the next time around in the reincarnation you will come back in a worse situation. If you end up in dire poverty and you are a dhali, in a ditch somewhere, no one will even bring you a cup of cold water because that is your kharma. They would be messing up what god's kharma is for you, even though god is not a personal god to the Hindu. You can see how it would be rather difficult to believe that God would want to heal you, especially if everything that is happening to you is the result of your kharma.

Islam has a very strong mindset of predeterminism. God causes everything. I have a friend who is from an Islamic background. He said that the problem with the religion of Islam is that they think they must earn god's favor, the reason being that Ishmael did not receive his father's blessing like Isaac did. It has always been this struggle to get god's favor. There is no grace in it. Islam is not a religion of grace. Is this Allah's will? It is kind of like a hyper-Calvinist.

However, in Christianity the very foundation is rooted in grace. When people can come into that understanding of grace, it actually makes it easier for them to receive their healing. Here is one of my favorite verses, 1 John 3:20. It is a powerful one. "Even if our hearts condemn us, God is greater than our heart." What is this verse saying? It is saying that God can forgive us when we cannot forgive our self.

Finding Grace

I did not understand that verse until 1994, when I was leading the Toronto meetings. During the daytime, I was going through inner healing with Carol Arnott and another gentleman. There were many badly broken areas in my life. Some of those areas of brokenness were also where I had the greatest fallings, weaknesses and failures. I did not understand it, never understood why I struggled with this, that and the other thing. Why was it so difficult to have victory in certain areas? Because I did not understand, I was very critical of myself and very judgmental of myself. I was my worst taskmaster. You can hide things from everybody but yourself. You cannot hide anything from yourself. It is all right in front of you, all the time, every thought, everything that should not be there.

Even though I did not understand what was happening, I would confess what the word said. I did not understand the word, but I believed it was true. Even if my heart condemns me, God is greater than my heart. I am forgiven. How many times can I be forgiven? Seventy times seven. Boy was I glad for that word!

Going through this inner healing, I got an insight into why I had been the way I was. Because I had not understood, I had thought that I had a weak will. All of a sudden I understood that it was not a matter of a weak will. My will was not nearly as free as I thought it was. There were subconscious drives, needs, wounds, pains and hurts that the enemy could so easily play on, causing me to go into tailspins. I didn't even know I had them or how they affected me. When all of this came into the light, something happened. My harshness toward myself was tempered. Before, I had thought that I was just making really bad choices and that I had a weak will. Now I was beginning to understand that I had demonic powers riding on the severe hurts and wounds that went back to before I was born. The enemy was using those things powerfully in my life.

When I came to understand that, it was so much easier for me to be merciful to myself, rather than being in that place where I had thought I was always making bad decisions. Then I knew how God could be so merciful. With the additional information, I was no longer so critical of myself. I realized that I was really carrying a bundle of problems around with me and that my will was not as free as I had thought. It became so much easier to be merciful and graceful toward myself. I had only just learned this but God knew this about me, better than anybody did. He fully understands our weaknesses, our drives, those subconscious things we are unaware of that prompt us to make bad choices. He understands it all. When I got that in my head, I understood that is why God can be so gracious and so merciful; because He knows and He understands.

Even when our hearts condemn us, God is greater than our hearts. That really began to hit home with me. By the way, a lot of my junk got cleaned up and I began to get a whole lot more victory.

For some of you, there is a spirit of rejection in operation in your life. My mother was conceived out of wedlock, my dad was conceived out of wedlock and I was conceived out of wedlock. You talk about a generational curse of rejection. My mother never could show affection to her mother, even to the day her mother died. I remember as a little boy that my mother told me, "Oooh! My little sister would get in bed with mom and let mom hold her. Oooh! I can't understand how she could do that." My mother never let her mother hold her. My mother could never receive affection from her mother. Of course, it was worse for her because Grandpa married Grandma two months before mom was born. My mother was carrying a whole lot more shame than I was.

I never understood why I could not let my mother kiss me. I still did not understand why at 42 years old. I had no recollection of ever allowing my mother to kiss me or to hold me, just like she couldn't let her mother hold or kiss her. Then all of a sudden, I got the understanding. I forgave mom and dad and all the other stuff that went with it. As it came to mind, I would forgive them. This was the fruit of healing.

When I went home and saw my mother, for the first time in her life I kissed her. For the first time in her life, I was a 42 year old man, and I allowed her to kiss me and hold me. But when I was a little boy, I could never understand why, when my mother drew close to me, I would back away when she wanted to kiss me. She would kiss my brother and my sister, but when she came to me, I would not allow it to happen. Until I discovered what the root was.

Conclusion

Now I have some good news for you. God understands. Some of you have trouble with intimacy. You can work hard for God and you can serve God, but when it comes to being intimate with God, you get shook up. If you never get healed of it, and I hope you will, but even if you don't, know that He loves you! And He knows why you can't be intimate with Him. He would like to heal you. I just want to encourage you. No religion has this grace other than Christianity, because He came and He bore our sicknesses and our diseases. He carried our pains as well as our sins and iniquities. Our healing is in the atonement. His shed blood forgives our sings. His wounded body heals our body and soul. Because He has done it, we can come boldly to the Throne of God in our time of need, to obtain mercy and help.

The Power of the Lord's Supper

This message on the Lord's Supper is the message I get more hugs and kisses from and more hate mail from than any other one message that I give. When I teach this message on communion I never tell the pastor beforehand what I am going to teach so that the congregation cannot blame their pastor for what I teach. I say this to save the pastor's reputation. The congregation cannot be mad at him for anything I say because he has not been informed prior to the service. He is innocent. If they want to be upset, they can be upset with me. Usually when I get a mean email or letter, it is because I have been misunderstood, so I will try to be clearer about what I am saying and what I am not saying.

Ecumenism of the Spirit

We can have an appreciation for the beliefs and traditions

of other people even when we may not totally agree with them. We can respect them. So you need to know that I have respect for the whole church. I love the whole church and I love anybody who is in love with Jesus.

There are people who have been born-again who have never heard the word "born-again." That just is not part of their Christian heritage. I learned early on, when I was nineteen or twenty years old and took my first full-time church, that there were people in it that did not come from a Baptist background like I did, but they knew Jesus. They were His disciples. They loved Him and they knew Him. And when I talked to them about Jesus I could see it in their eyes, that they really did know Him.

Nevertheless, there were also people in that church, who were leaders in the church who, in my opinion, were not saved. They didn't really know Jesus. They went to church for the wrong reasons. Their hearts were cold. But I think that can be true in any tradition, any denomination.

I was talking to a priest once in Australia, a Catholic priest. Growing up mostly in Protestant churches, I knew that twenty percent of the people give eighty percent of the money. Twenty percent of the church's members do eighty percent of the work. The other eighty percent of the people give twenty percent of the money and do twenty percent of the work. I was shocked when the priest told me, "Do you know that in our parish twenty percent of the people give eighty percent of the money and twenty percent of our members carry eighty percent of the work of the church." All of a sudden I realized that the level of commitment in the Catholic Church was about the same as the level of commitment in the Baptist church.

I've learned that often we compare the best in our tradition with the worst in others' traditions and that's not fair. I want the prayer of Jesus to be answered; that we would realize that we are brothers and sisters, all of us who know Jesus and know the Father through Him. Even though we may have some differences in doctrine and some differences in practice, there may even be some things where we disagree with each other, we are all counted as Christians because we all believe the same things. I believe we are counted as Christians because we know Jesus. We've accepted Him. We believe in Him. We are trusting in Him.

I want to share my own spiritual pilgrimage in the area of working toward Christian unity; unity that is not based on compromising what we believe, so that we do not water down our beliefs until they become meaningless. Instead, I have what I call ecumenism of the spirit. The word ecumenism is based on a word that means "coming together in unity, in an ecumenical spirit where we honor each other."

This desire for unity is not about us all becoming one church. I think that is not going to happen, short of the Second Coming of Jesus. We are one church, the universal church, but we are currently divided around doctrines and practices. We can honor each other as part of the Body of Christ even though we may not be part of the same denomination or the same local church. Jesus prayed that we would be one, even as He and the Father were one.

I believe that the Father, the Son and the Holy Spirit in their counsel determined that they would give us two major signs of unity that would bind all Christians together. No matter where we go in the world, these would be our points of unity – baptism and communion. The enemy likes to work at hurting the heart of God, so two of the biggest points of disunity among Christians are baptism and communion, or the Lord's Supper as it is also called. It is actually over the issue of the Lord's Supper that Protestants and Catholics have been unable to come together.

Five Views of the Lord's Supper

When I was in my last Baptist church, I realized that my view of communion really was not a Baptist view of communion. I grew up in the Baptist church. We had communion once every three months or quarterly. Other Baptist churches had it semi-annually, and some Presbyterian churches, historically speaking, only had communion once a year. One of the reasons the communion services were so infrequent was because the Catholic Church had communion every week. At one time, anything that was considered Catholic, Protestants did not want to have anything to do with.

When I was in seminary, twenty-two to twenty-five years old, one day I was out looking around the campus. Mind you, it was the second largest seminary in the world and it had the largest theological library in the world. I looked all around the campus but I couldn't find a cross on any of the buildings. I asked a professor about this issue. I told him I had looked at the chapel and at the other buildings and I could not find one cross anywhere. But there were little Grecian urns everywhere. I asked him why. I told him that was weird to me. His response was that because the Catholic Church has crosses on top of their churches and buildings, we did not. That was astounding to me.

Another time I asked him about the chapel services; why they always said, "Let us stand to pray." I asked him why it was that we did not kneel. Again his response was because the Catholics knelt in their services. I thought that made no sense. So what?

In the Baptist church, we have to be baptized by immersion to be a member of the church. It is supposed to be our profession of faith and it should happen shortly after the salvation experience. That is my personal belief. It is not good Baptist doctrine. Let me give you an example why. There was a young woman in my church who wanted to join the church. She was Methodist. She was already a key leader. I needed her to be able to have more responsibility but she couldn't until she became a member. She had become a Christian as a teenager and been baptized by sprinkling as her profession of faith, right after she was saved.

Our denomination said that her baptism wasn't a real baptism and that it wouldn't work according to the doctrine of the Baptist church. We told her that before she could become a member of our church she had to be baptized by immersion. She met with me and this is what she told me. "I'm going to do it, just to meet your rule, but you need to know that this will not be my baptism. I'm just going through the motions to join the church. My real baptism will always be the one right after I was saved, when I was sprinkled, because that was my profession of faith."

I didn't ever want to do that again, to force people to jump through hoops for a ritual that doesn't mean anything to them. That just did not set well with me. I did not like that at all. I started a group called the "Adult Inquiry Group." We held it one night a week for four weeks. We studied the basics of the faith. People would describe their spiritual pilgrimages the first night. Some would start crying because most of the people in the group weren't saved or they were backslidden. If they were Christians, they definitely were not the kind of Christian that we had in our church. They were in culture shock. When people first came to our church they were so shocked by the way we worshipped that they could not do anything but watch.

The second week we talked about what it meant to be a Christian? How does one become a Christian? What is our part? What is Jesus' part? What He has done and what are we to do? The third week we talked about baptism and the Lord's Supper. The last week we talked about what would happen if someone went to a new city and started a new church. What would they want? What would they look for in the people who they would like to join their church? In other words, what does the lifestyle of a committed Christian look like? I had to think through all these things myself.

On the night we talked about baptism and the Lord's Supper, when it came to the part about the Lord's Supper, I would teach them that there are basically five views of the Lord's Supper.

First, there is the Quaker view which is that we don't need to do communion anymore. Quakers do not believe in baptism or the Lord's Supper. That is the lowest view.

Secondly, we have the Baptist view. The Baptist view is that the Lord's Supper is an ordinance, something Jesus ordered us to do. If we are going to be obedient we need to do it but it has no benefit other than obeying an ordinance. There is no power and no grace communicated to us through the Lord's Supper. The bread and wine of communion are just symbols. In the Baptist and Pentecostal churches, we see this low view of communion as far as relationship to the presence of Jesus. They also believe that when communion is over, the leftover elements are thrown into the trash can.

Thirdly, Lutherans have yet another view of communion. The Lutheran view is called consubstantiation meaning the presence of Jesus is with, over, under and around the very elements of the Lord's Supper, the bread and the wine.

Fourthly, the Catholics, the Orthodox and the Coptic views take communion a step further. They believe in transubstantiation meaning that the bread and the wine become in substance, but not appearance, the body and blood of Jesus; that a conversion takes place as one substance changes into another.

Fifthly, there is the Presbyterian reformed view, which believes that the person who comes in faith can expect to meet the real presence of Jesus in communion.

I think it is sad that the word transubstantiation came about and that the church tried to explain the mystery. As we tried to explain the confession of the church, the belief of the church, and the mystery, which hadn't been tried in early church history; in our explanations, divisions arose.

It was Thomas Aquinas in the 11th Century who gave definition to what had always been conceived as a mystery, a supernatural mystery that wasn't understood. In his work Summa Contra Gentiles written in 1264, Aquinas said this, "The Body and Blood of Christ is not affected by the accidents of the bread and wine. It is not impossible that divine power can affect the subject without changing the nature of the accidents. In this sacrament He conserves the accident while changing the substance." The term 'accidents' is used here in the Aristotelian sense that, "accidents are the perceptible qualities or properties of an object such as its color, texture, size, shape, etc. as contrasted with the substance in which it inheres."

Now prior to the 11th Century it was believed and confessed that Jesus said, "This is My body, this is My blood." It wasn't understood in what way or how this happened; whether it was around the bread and wine or whether the inner substance actually changed. There was no understanding like that. Nevertheless, with new definitions came divisions.

It was at this point that I realized I had acquired a Presbyterian view of communion. To me there is a time that we should expect to experience the presence of Jesus during the act of communion. At that time, I had a higher view than the Baptists did so, when I was pastoring the Baptist church I went to the deacons and asked how often they would consent to let me do communion. I wanted to do it more often than the Baptist tradition called for, and I wanted to show a biblical basis for it. I don't think you can find any place in the New Testament to indicate how often the early church took communion, but if you go back to the church fathers you will find those men who were discipled by one of the twelve apostles. That's getting pretty close. You will find in their writings that they took communion every Sunday when the church gathered.

A Church for People Who Don't Go to Church

Now God called me to St Louis to start a church. Understand that if the Pope comes to the United States to visit, he will often go to St Louis. It is not because there are more Catholics in St Louis than in any other city, but because there are more practicing Catholics in St Louis than in any city in the United States. About one in two people that you meet in St Louis are probably Roman Catholic. It has the most committed Catholic community of any city in the United States. It is here that God sent me to St Louis to start a church. Even though the city has the highest proportion of practicing Catholics of any city in the United States, it still has a lot of backslidden Catholics that drop out of the church in their teenage years. I felt like the Lord said, "You start a church with people who don't go to church. Don't try to take people out of another church."

We began our church. We had eleven people in the church to begin with. We didn't have a building. We were not even meeting on Sundays. We were just meeting in our homes and at that time, we had only one home that we were meeting in. It took me eleven months to gather those first eleven people. I was a very successful church planter!

I didn't know a soul in St. Louis. I was working in 80 different stores all over Illinois, Missouri and one in Kansas. I was gone a lot and it was hard to meet people while trying to raise my family and make some money. It was not an easy time. John Wimber was right when he said planting a church would be the hardest thing I would ever do in my life. It was also the most rewarding.

One time a handful of us in the church called about 20,000 people, telling them that we were starting a new church for people that had no church and that we wanted to be a church for people who didn't like "normal" church. We said that we wanted our new church to be "real" and that we were against hypocrisy. We asked if they had a church and if not, would they be interested in coming to our church. This was a bit of a different approach.

We were a mix of denominations. There was Paul from Washington State who was a Lutheran, and Nicholas who was Greek Orthodox, and Gary, a heathen in the bars until he was saved. When I led him to the Lord, he was kind of a New Age heathen. And Kathleen who had sung for the Pope in the Sistine Chapel. We had German Catholics and Italian Catholics, one Presbyterian guy and the rest were Southern Baptist. And then there was me, right out of the Baptist church. Our first little group was kind of a takeover of a Baptist Bible study.

Learning to Honor One Another

When I went to St Louis I had to decide if the new church I was starting would be a church for Baptists that got filled with the Spirit then were kicked out of the church, or if it was going to be more than that? I told the Lord I wanted to do a great experiment. I wanted to see if we could find unity in the Lord; unity in the Holy Spirit that would overcome our doctrinal differences. I wanted to see if we could honor the differences in our traditions and never coerce any of the people who would come to our church. If they wanted to baptize their babies, they would be free to do it as long as I was free to refrain from being the one to baptize the baby. If they believed in transubstantiation or consubstantiation or real presence or that the elements were just a symbol that would be up to them. I would tell them what I believed and they would be free to believe what they believed. But all of us would take communion together. We had some challenges.

In the beginning, I gathered together my congregation of eleven people and we did communion. I wanted to build the model of weekly communion into the DNA of the church so that it would be in place when we grew. Every time we met we did communion.

Well, we were doing our first communion in the house of the Southern Baptist. After communion was over, Helen and Donna were on their way with the communion leftovers to the waste can when Nicholas saw them. Being Greek Orthodox and believing that when I had prayed the prayer of consecration over the elements they were no longer crackers and wine but had become the body and blood of Jesus, Nicholas stood up between them and said, "What are you doing?" I saw the problem we were facing and I thought, "This is a teachable moment."

At that point in the life of our church I had not yet taught on communion. What I had taught was the five differing views of communion. I asked Helen and Donna if they believed that God had brought Nicholas into our church and they responded, "Yes," and that they loved Nicholas. Then I asked Nick if he believed that God had brought Helen and Donna into our fellowship. He also responded, "Yes," and said that they had been like second mothers to him since his mother had died a few years prior to this.

Then I asked how we might be able to work this out in light of what all three had just testified to. I knew that the Holy Spirit was taking care of this issue. Helen and Donna then asked Nick what they did in the Greek Orthodox tradition with the leftover communion elements. His response was that they consumed them; they drank the leftover wine and ate the leftover bread, all of it. Helen and Donna agreed to that and asked Nicholas to help them. For sixteen years after that night nothing was ever thrown away.

I told Nicholas that I was not asking him to believe as Helen and Donna believed and I was not asking Helen and Donna to believe what Nicholas believed. I was asking each of them to find a way to walk this issue out agreeably, as brothers and sisters in Christ, in honor and love as one fellowship. They were able to honor one another.

Nicholas became our first missionary and became a full time teacher at YWAM, teaching in Guatemala. His sister became the second full time missionary from our church. She also became a leader at YWAM in Texas.

Right before this challenge over communion, we had a challenge with Paul who was basically adopted by Bill and Helen, the Southern Baptist couple at whose house we did a lot of our meetings. He came in one night and he was fit–

to be-tied because he had just heard about eternal security; once saved always saved. He had never heard that before. He did not know that Bill had been a deacon in the Southern Baptist church and that eternal security was one of his most cherished doctrines. Paul came in, we were talking, and he told me that he had just found out that very day that there were people who believed that once you were saved you were always saved, that they could do whatever they wanted and still get to Heaven. He said he thought that was cheap grace and wondered how anyone could believe in that.

At the break time, I went over to Paul and all I said was that Bill and Helen, the owners of the house where we were meeting, his "adopted" mother and father believe in eternal security. I told Paul that I was not asking him to believe this doctrine. I said that was not important to me. I said that what was important to me was that he think about what he had said and the way he had said it. I left it at that and went to get a drink. When I came back there was Paul right in front of Bill and Helen, on his knees crying and asking them to forgive him for his abrasive attitude. His doctrine had not changed but he was learning how to honor brothers and sisters in Christ who held different traditions. We do not have to be in agreement in order to honor one another.

Later when we had our own building and had about 400 congregants, sometimes the amount of leftover elements would be challenging to consume. It was time for another meeting. We called in the person with the Roman Catholic background and asked him what they did in the Roman Catholic Church with their leftovers. He said they saved them and used them again at a later date. Nicholas was in agreement and so that became our process.

Because of all this, I cannot throw the elements away anymore. I just can't. I don't believe in transubstantiation, but I wish I could because I think its better. Doctrinally I don't know if it is really better, but I do think it would make communion more special to all of us.

Communion as a Channel of Grace

Before I went to St Louis, I knew I was moving to the most Catholic city in America. That was my mission field. I also knew that my view of communion as a Baptist was pretty low. Not much was expected from the Baptist viewpoint. As I studied and read church history I said to the Lord that, "if one receives a prophet in the name of a prophet, he receives a prophet's reward," so that if I were to receive communion as nothing more than "an order," then that is all I can expect to receive from it. But if I receive communion as a channel of grace, then I believe I will receive grace. Now my personal view is the Presbyterian view, that when you come to communion in faith, not mechanically, you should expect to experience the actual presence of Jesus. And I believe like Wesley and the Methodists believe that participating in communion is a way of maintaining grace in our lives. It is also the means of maintaining the Baptism of the Spirit in our lives through the frequent participation in the act of communion.

I asked the Lord how we could do communion on a weekly basis without it becoming just another ritual. Now, in the Baptist church, every fifth Sunday, four times a year, someone would come and preach in my church and I would go to some other church. I would go to different denominations and I would watch how they conducted their services. I was curious. I wanted to know what other people were doing. I watched some that had communion every week. I did not think their communion services looked that meaningful. They looked ritualistic. I did not think they were expecting much from communion.

I went to the Lord and said that I wanted to do communion every week and I wanted it to be meaningful. It was my belief that the early church had communion every week. I could not prove it from the New Testament, but I could prove it from the disciples of the original disciples. That seemed authentic to me. I told the Lord that I wanted to be in the tradition that went back to the early church. My question was how were we going to do communion so that it would be meaningful and not become a dull ritual? I wanted it to be meaningful.

We did communion a couple of times and I think we came close to that point of grace. I just wanted to do what Jesus did and not try to explain it but leave it as mystery.

When we did communion we had one person would hold the tray and another who would hold the bread. The people would kneel and pray then they would come up front. The person with the tray of bread would say, "Jesus said, 'This is My body, take and eat'." And when they came with the tray of juice they would say, "Jesus said, 'This cup is the new covenant in My blood which is shed for many for the remission of sin'." All we were doing was quoting Jesus. We did not try to explain it. I just wanted us to confess the mystery.

When I had other people who came on my staff in the Vineyard in St. Louis, people who came from all different denominational backgrounds (Presbyterian, Baptists, etc.) one of my instructions to them was that I did not want them to say, "This cup symbolizes" or, "This bread symbolizes." Jesus did not say that. I told them they were to quote what Jesus said at the first communion. They were not to try to explain it or to define it; just quote what Jesus said and leave it as a mystery. I knew that if we were encouraging a low view, we would get a low view blessing.

I remembered that when I was sixteen I was dating a girl whose brother was a preacher. He was the first preacher I had ever met that believed in praying for the sick. He was Methodist. One day we went to a Holiness camp meeting. They had a preacher and evangelist who did communion that day. He blessed the elements with the people standing there. He told them to pray, to get right with God and to be thankful for what God had done in their lives. Then when they were ready to take communion, if the people would lift their heads up, someone would come around to each individual and would give them communion. They just received the grace.

I'll never forget the first time I read John 6. Jesus said that we have to eat His flesh and drink His blood. If we do not, we do not have any part in Him. Many of His disciples left Him at that point. He asked the twelve disciples if they were going to leave Him also. He knew that what He was saying was a very difficult thing. I do not think the disciples understood what He was saying, but they said, "Where else are we going to go? You have the words of life" (John 6:68).

What am I saying? I am saying that I want us to experience more from communion than we may have previously. And I hope I can get us to have a higher view of the power of grace.

The Power of Grace

In Australia recently, as I was getting ready to preach this same sermon, someone brought a cloth up to me, right before I started the sermon. The person asked me to bless the cloth. The intention was for healing based on Acts 19 where they took sweat bands from Paul and people were healed. Before long people brought up everything. It was a God set–up; I would not have been smart enough to do it myself. They brought up their wallets, they brought up their shoes, their socks, their clothes; anything. I had a huge stack of clothes. It was something to see.

I remember that when I started out I said, "I know what you believe. You believe that these cloths can carry anointing. You believe that these cloths, all the things you have put up here, can be saturated with the very presence of God. You believe that these things can be a channel of blessing, carrying healing anointing to people. That's why you brought them up to the front. You are believing for me to bless them and pray over them. You are believing and going to carry them back to the sick. You believe that these things have now become channels of grace. If you can believe that, why can't you believe that when we bless the elements of the Lord's Supper they can become channels of grace; that His presence can impregnate them just as it does the cloths, and that they will bring grace?"

For a Protestant, the most important part of the service is the sermon because Protestants believe that through the preaching of the Word salvation is offered and is received. In the Catholic and the Orthodox traditions the most important thing that happens in the service is the consecration of the elements of the Lord's Supper. It is believed that through the elements grace, power, healing and forgiveness are communicated. This is ongoing forgiveness.

I would be so bold as to say that when we preach this concept it is like hearing the gospel on the radio. When we participate in the Lord's Supper it is like watching the gospel on interactive television. It involves all our senses, not just our hearing. It involves our sight, our taste, our smell, our touch. It's real. And it is not just about getting saved. It is about how to live once we are saved, about how to have better families and raise kids and all the stuff that goes with normal church life. Not all sermons have the full gospel in them but if we do communion every week, no matter what else is preached that day, we have declared the gospel in the words of institution.

Evangelism through Communion

I began to see how to use communion evangelistically. Wesley used it evangelistically too. After one song in the service, I would get up and declare that we were about to partake of the Lord's Supper. Then we would begin with me blessing the elements. I would pray a prayer of consecration over the elements and then our worship team would lead us into worship. I would invite anyone present who knew the Lord to come forward and participate in the Lord's Supper. I would tell them this was not a Vineyard supper, this was not a Catholic supper, and this was not a Baptist supper, but that this was the Lord's Supper. I made it clear that anyone who knew the Lord Jesus Christ was invited to participate. I would remind them that the Apostle Paul told us we were first to examine ourselves. If we were living in rebellion and sin, rebellion against God, then participating in the Lord's Supper was not going to automatically bring us grace while we are walking in rebellion. We always need to examine ourselves first and acknowledge any unconfessed sin in our lives, any bitterness and any resentment. We then need to take care of those issues first. Come up to the altar, the communion rail, and get right with God first, then take communion.

When we started in the school, we did not have a nice railing to kneel in front of. We were in a gymnasium. We had tables but they didn't even have any tablecloths on them. In the Baptist church, we had nice stainless steel or gold-plated trays with the little cups and we had the nice trays for the bread. And we had a big brass cross that was always on the communion table. It said "This do in remembrance of Me" across the front of the table. In the gym, we didn't have any of that. I knew that we had to put something that was not in the Bible and that was outside of all the traditions of the church on our communion table. And it wasn't a brass cross.

We did not own one; we could not afford one. Instead, we put a Kleenex® box on the communion table. We saw so many people weeping at the communion rail that we had to put Kleenex® out for them.

Now that I wasn't a Baptist, we started using wine instead of grape juice but that didn't work since so many of our new converts were recovering alcoholics and drug addicts. We had to go back to grape juice. However, I want to tell you something; it worked!

The two most prominent things that caused people to come under conviction were the consecration of the elements of communion and the words of institution, partaken of every Sunday and combined with the passionate worship of the people. These people were used to going to dead churches where people were not really into worship. The only people singing would be the choir. Everybody else would be looking through their purses, impatient to get to the sermon. When people came into our church, everybody was alive, everybody was worshipping. The people were passionate for Jesus in worship. When they heard the words of institution before the worship began, God used the Gospel. It got people's attention.

I grew up in the Baptist church and we had seen plenty of baptisms, but this was new in church for almost all of our new converts in St. Louis. The first time we had a baptism I couldn't believe what was happening. It was so "unreligious." It was so unreligious it almost seemed irreverent. I was used to quietness with maybe someone saying "Amen" during a baptism. For our first baptism we borrowed someone's church. We had about 13 people to baptize. When the first one went under, and most of our congregation were new Christians, they began to scream and holler joyfully, jumping up and down, quite unrestrained. I was thinking,

"Wow, they're actually excited about this." For sixteen years, every time we did a baptism, everyone would stand up and cheer and clap. My goal was reached. Regardless of what they believed doctrinally, they had learned to expect that if they acted in faith and sincerity, with expectation, that grace would come to them.

I would teach people that when they would go to the communion table, if there was anything wrong, they were to confess it first and ask God to forgive them. I taught that they could also pray: "Lord, as I take of communion, would You let grace and power come into me. As these elements have been consecrated, they are holy unto You. As I take them, would You make me a holy vessel unto You. This is now meant to be a blessing to me, would you make me a blessing in this world this week."

This was all so exciting to me. I tell you, it is better to have a baby than to try to raise the dead, which is just another way of saying that church planting is more fun than taking over a dead church.

Once, when I was a young pastor in a Baptist church I had a conversation with an older man from Australia who was very well respected. We were talking together about what I believed; something to do with communion. He said, "You know, Randy, you have a phenomenal, logical approach to communion." That comment surprised me and I told him that I did not even know what he meant by that comment. He responded that what he meant was that I was more concerned about the reality of the experience than I was the doctrine behind the Lord's Supper. He said he could see that I wanted the communion experience to be real, to experience the real presence of Jesus during the communion observance. That excited me because that was exactly where my heart was. I want to feel His presence.

Later, as I studied church history, I found that there were people who would go to the deathly ill, taking the host (bread) from the Sacristy (which is the room in the church that houses the sacred vessels, and vestments and elements) and rub the host all over the bodies of the sick and the sick would be healed! Smith Wigglesworth got hold of this principle. He took communion every day and he was Pentecostal. The gospel on the radio and the gospel on television, it's still the gospel. There is not a purer gospel than the words of institution. And no matter what else you preach, if you have had communion, those who you preach to have heard the essence of the gospel message.

Praying the Prayer of Institution

When I pray the prayer of institution, I use the words from Matthew rather than Corinthians. In Matthew 26, Jesus is instituting the Lord's Supper.

Matthew 26:27-28 (NKJV)

[27] Then He took the cup, and gave thanks, and gave it to them, saying, "Drink from it, all of you. [28] For this is My blood of the new covenant, which is shed for many for the remission of sins."

Now, I Corinthians 11:23-30 (NKJV)

[23] For I received from the Lord that which I also delivered to you: that the Lord Jesus on the same night in which He was betrayed took bread; [24] and when He had given thanks, He broke it and said, "Take, eat; this is My body which is broken for you; do this in remembrance of Me." [25] In the same manner He also took the cup after supper, saying, "This cup is the new covenant in My blood.

This do, as often as you drink it, in remembrance of Me."

²⁶ *For as often as you eat this bread and drink this cup, you proclaim the Lord's death till He comes.*

²⁷ *Therefore whoever eats this bread or drinks this cup of the Lord in an unworthy manner will be guilty of the body and blood of the Lord.* ²⁸ *But let a man examine himself, and so let him eat of the bread and drink of the cup.* ²⁹ *For he who eats and drinks in an unworthy manner eats and drinks judgment to himself, not discerning the Lord's body.* ³⁰ *For this reason many are weak and sick among you, and many sleep"*

The traditional Protestant understanding of verses 28-30 is in the context of I Corinthians chapters 11-14. Verses 29 and 30 indicate that during communion the people were not waiting on each other. They were taking communion in the middle of a love feast where they had other things to eat. Some were eating everything before others could get there. They were not honoring each other. People were not honoring one another as one body, and as a result of this unworthy behavior some got sick. That is the traditional Protestant understanding.

Healing through the Eucharist

There is another perspective on 1 Corinthians 11:29-30 that I want to share with you. It is a perspective I personally advocate and it is this: anyone who eats and drinks without recognizing the body of the Lord eats and drinks judgment on himself. That is why many of us are weak and sick and many have fallen asleep.

First, notice that this perspective is not about the cup. It is only the body, not the cup. I believe Paul is talking about the body. If we take communion without recognizing the body of our Lord, it can lead to judgment. That is why some have grown weak and sick and some have died.

Let me explain further what I think this perspective means. We believe and understand that Jesus said the cup is the new covenant in His blood which is shed for many for the remission of sins. We believe that. We know that we are forgiven our sins because of His shed blood. That has presented and communicated to us in the Lord's Supper by what He said. And so we have faith in His shed blood to bring forgiveness of our sins.

Now if the cup represents the blood and the forgiveness of sin, what is the body for? We know He bore our sicknesses and our diseases in His body. In the Hebrew, in Isaiah 53 verse 4, we see the same two Hebrew verbs: He carried our sins and bore our iniquity. Those are the exact same verbs that said our sicknesses and our pain.

When we do not discern what happened at the cross in the body of Jesus for our healing, we do not discern the body in the sense of "as I take communion I am reminded that in His body He bore my disease. In His body, He bore my sicknesses. In His body, He bore my sorrows." The word "sorrows" in the King James is way too weak. It doesn't mean "sorrow or sadness". Everywhere else in the Old Testament and in the New Testament, it means "sicknesses." The word "sorrows" is also a word for "pain." In Matthew's Gospel, the Septuagint version was quoted, which is the Greek version of the Old Testament. Matthew Chapter 8, verse 17 in the NIV says:

[17] This is fulfilled that which was spoken by the prophet Isaiah, 'He took up our infirmities and carried our diseases.'

If we understand that in His blood is forgiveness of sin, and every time we take communion we are reminded of that, then we understand that it causes us to have faith in His blood. If we discern that in His body He died, bearing our sicknesses and diseases so that we can be healed, then we can receive the grace for healing.

I want to challenge every one of you, regardless of the church you come from, to discern the body of Christ in communion, to understand what it means, and to appropriate by faith the healing that is provided for us in the Lord's Supper.

The Eucharist as Celebration and Thanksgiving

Now the Catholic word for the Lord's Supper is Eucharist. Eucharist is a Greek word which means celebration, thanksgiving. It gets closer to the real meaning of communion which is celebrating thanksgiving. In the early church, for the first one thousand years, the emphasis was not on Jesus' death. The emphasis was on His resurrection. For the first thousand years of Christianity, the emphasis was not about His death so that we could go to Heaven. That was believed and that was true. The early church understood that. Paul was the one who wrote about it. Nevertheless, the greater emphasis was that we were saved by His life because Jesus was raised from the dead. He defeated the devil. He defeated demons. He defeated disease. He defeated death.

The early gospel was considered what they called Christus Victor, which refers to a Christian understanding of the atonement that views Christ's death as the means by which the powers of evil that held humankind under their dominion were defeated. It is a model for the atonement that dates to the Church Fathers and was a dominant theory of the atonement for a thousand years. The preachers would say, "Jesus was killed." We tried to kill Him, but God raised Him from the dead! And God has given Him victory and He is our Victor. And in Him we have victory! We have power over demons. We have power over diseases. We have power over damnation. We have been set free! He is our Victor. This is good news!

Think of it in this way; if the emphasis is on His death so that we can go to Heaven, we can be guilty of preaching pie-in-the-sky, in the sweet-by-and-by. It's true; I thank God that I'm going to Heaven. I thank God for eternal life. But, I thank God also, that in preaching of the gospel, He is Victor and that victory starts right now. I don't have to wait until I get to Heaven to have the benefit of His death because He is risen. He is not dead.

When we take communion we proclaim His death until He comes because He is no longer dead. He is alive! When we take communion, we come to a celebration. We should not play sad songs for communion. This is a celebration. This is our thanksgiving. This is to remind us that He did bear our sins. He did die in our place. And He did bear our diseases. He has victory over all of these things for us. We can participate in His victory. It's His life. As we come with gratitude and thanksgiving and humbly admit, "I forsake all other righteousness except that which is in Him," we are looking to the cross. We are looking to His death. We are looking to His blood for forgiveness. We are looking at His body for our healing. We are celebrating the gospel. When we believe that, we have great hope.

If we don't discern what He did in His body, then we do not have a very high view of communion or of healing. For a long time the church has really only understood the cup. It is time we understood the body too. We can get excited about taking communion when we understand the cup and the bread. I have seen people slain in the spirit during communion. They had to be pulled out of the way. That excites me but not nearly as much as when I see people healed when they take communion.

To those who come with understanding, discerning the body and all that He did for us, we should expect healing to happen in communion. Until that happens, we do not yet fully understand with faith what He did for us. We are not yet discerning the body of Jesus.

Freedom in Christ

What do I mean when I speak of consecrating the elements? Consecration means to make something or someone holy. The reason I like to use the word consecrate is that I like to follow by saying, "Lord, as you consecrate these elements, make them channels of blessing and grace to us. We also consecrate ourselves to you. Make us channels of blessing and grace in the world this week."

Some people don't like the word consecrate; they think it's too strong a word. So if you don't like the word, then just think of it as blessing the elements.

Right before I consecrate the elements of the Lord's Supper there is one other thing I like to do. I have to warn you, I'm eclectic. That means that I draw from many sources. If I see something I like in the history of the church, I will take it for myself. I will not let anyone else's view prejudice my enjoyment of being in God's presence.

Before I consecrate the elements I like to make the sign of the cross over myself. And I don't know exactly which way we are supposed to do it, but I actually cross myself. Why? Am I Catholic? No, I have only been in the Catholic Church once in my lifetime. Then why do I do it? Because it feels good. I like it! Why should I be robbed of something that I enjoy. It makes the ordinance more meaningful for me. I know Christians have done this for hundreds of years, maybe over a thousand years, several thousand perhaps. Please don't be offended if I do this. Give me the freedom to do this and I will give you the freedom to not do it.

I looked back to the third and fourth centuries of church history and I read about the sign of the cross. Some people were relieved of their sickness and disease, some were not. The same is true about people who had hands laid on them to receive or be baptized in the Spirit. Some received and spoke in tongues and some did not. The implications were that it was still happening even though it was not happening to everybody. This would mean that sign of the cross may not relieve everyone from their sicknesses and diseases, but it was working for some. So, why not do it? There is some benefit.

Once I did a service in Alaska. One of the guys teaching on deliverance was Catholic. He teaches on deliverance all over the world. He had been trained by Pablo Bottari and he had taken the Protestant practice of deliverance and was using it in the Catholic Church all over the world. His name is Neal Lozano. He wrote a book called Unbound: A Practical Guide to Deliverance. I went up to him and I said, "Neal, I know you are Catholic. I know that your church law says that you can't take communion with us. But I just want you to know that I am inviting you to take communion with us. You are welcome to, as my brother in the Lord."

He said, "Thank you, Randy. I appreciate your heart, but I can't." I told him that I understood but that I wanted to make sure that he felt welcome to participate in the communion service.

In this service we consecrated the elements and the people began taking communion. One of the people spilled his cup, right onto the floor. People walked by and did not see it. They just walked through it, stepped in it and just kept going. I watched Neal. I saw tears running down his face. He took his handkerchief out of his pocket, got on his knees and wiped up every little drop, ever so reverently.

Now my view and Neal's view are probably not exactly alike but I understand one thing. For him, communion has a lot of meaning. I actually wish I could have such a high view of the Lord's Supper. But I thank God that I have a higher view than I used to have. You do not have to feel guilty if you don't. I am not asking anyone to switch his or her view. I am just recounting my progress, my pilgrimage and what has been meaningful to me.

When I give communion, I always invite everyone who has been born again and knows Jesus to take communion with us. I begin by consecrating the elements and then we move into worship. I like to keep the front area empty so that people can come up and have freedom to worship. I do not want to do anything to compromise worship. I have seen people waving swords, people waving flags and people jumping and shouting during the service as communion is going on.

Once, I had a guy in our church, an Apache Indian; he really was a full-blooded Apache Indian. And when he got saved . . . and he was a fighter, a brawler, a drunkard, a womanizer. When he got saved, he really got saved. The only problem was that he had a tendency to sit behind the visitors and when he got really excited, instead of saying, "Amen!" he would let out a very loud war whoop. You could see those visitors all but jump out of their skins.

Once a month we had this meeting where the visitors would come. They would come up wanting to know about the war whoop thing going on in our church. I would tell them that it was Tony Sanchez, that he was a full-blooded Apache Indian. He had formerly been a womanizer; he stole, he was a brawler, and he fought. He hadn't been a good father; he had not been a good husband. Then he got gloriously saved. You would see him carrying his kids on his shoulders. He became a good man. All of his previous behavior had changed dramatically. He would get so happy because of what Jesus had done for him. Occasionally, he would have to let out a war whoop. The very people who were at first scared and offended, the next time he did it, they would look and you could see tears running down their cheeks. Then I got pastoral wisdom and I asked Tony to sit up on the front row with me. In the early years in our church, you had to run the gauntlet to get to the communion rail!

I think it is important not to rush when we come to the communion table. I invite everyone to go and spend a little time when they come up for communion. If they want to kneel, they can kneel. I like to kneel. I don't care if Catholics kneel. I like to kneel. I like to thank Him because this is a time for thanksgiving. I come to the Lord's Supper with thanksgiving. I think about all that He has purchased for me and all that He has done for me. I remind myself of this every time I take communion. I thank Him myself for what He did in His body. I thank Him for what He did with His blood. I appropriate these things for myself.

After I take the communion, I stay a little longer and I thank Him again. I just give Him a little bit of time for a visitation. Then I get up and make room for someone else. I urge people not to hurry and not to line up but just to keep the altar area full.

There are certain songs that I like better than others for communion. I prefer the more intimate songs for myself. I don't mind a more lively song at the start of communion but I like it when the music begins to quiet down. Not that it should be quiet the whole time. I am just trying to say that if we are going to do communion on a weekly basis, we cannot have just one special song to do during communion every week. We need a variety. Whether communion is a time of celebration or intimacy, it is always a time of thanksgiving. I pray that as we take communion we discern the benefits of His body. I am not going to try to explain it in the words of institution. I am so thankful because I just want to quote what He said:

> *"On the night that our Lord was betrayed, He took the bread and He blessed it. And He gave it to His disciples and He said, 'This is My body which is given for you'." Luke 22:19*

> *"And after the supper, after He had, in the middle of the supper, gotten up and clothed Himself as a servant and washed the very feet of His disciples, He returned to the table and He took the cup and He blessed it and He gave it to His disciples and He said, 'This cup is the new covenant in My blood which is shed for many for the remission of sins.'" Matthew 26: 27-28*

The Apostle Paul said that as often as we eat of this bread and drink of this cup, we proclaim the Lord's death until He comes.

Randy's Prayer for Consecration of the Elements for Communion

"Father, in Jesus' name I ask you to consecrate the bread that is on these plates. And I pray that there would be a miracle; that You would so penetrate and be so be present with this bread, that You would make it channels of grace that would bring healing to bodies. And I ask, Lord, that in the name of Jesus, You would also consecrate the fruit of the vine in these cups. Lord, we pray in Jesus' name that You would cause us to appropriate the forgiveness of our sins and the forgiveness of our shortcomings. As we take of this cup, we would meditate on and remember what He did for us. I pray, Lord that we would leave with a sense of fresh cleansing and fresh grace. I ask, God, that You would make this celebration, this thanksgiving of Your Son's victory on our behalf, meaningful to us; that we would feel the Holy Spirit touching us. And as we kneel humbly before these communion rails and tables, that You would hear our prayers of thanksgiving for what You have done for us. For we celebrate in Thee our victory which reminds us of His death and His resurrection on our behalf. Lord, I pray that you would also consecrate every believer that comes forward. God, would you make them a gospel this week? Would You make them a good news this week wherever they are working, where they are at? Would You empower them with boldness and grace and love? Would You make us more like Jesus? In His name we pray. Amen."

References

Aquinas, St. Thomas. (1264). Summa Contra Gentiles. Book 4, Chapters 61 to 69

Aulen, Gustaf. (2003). Christus Victor: An Historical Study of the Three Main Types of the Idea of Atonement.

Brown, Driver and Briggs. (1996). Brown-Driver-Briggs Hebrew and English Lexicon. Hendrickson Publishers; Peabody, MA .

Eugene, OR: Wipf & Stock Publishers

Other books by Randy Clark

Healing Unplugged

Essential Guide to Healing

Entertaining Angels

There Is More

Power, Holiness and Evangelism

Lighting Fires

Changed in a Moment

Training Manuals Available

Ministry Team Training Manual

Schools of Healing and Impartation Workbooks

Core Message Series

Words of Knowledge

Biblical Basis of Healing

Baptism in the Holy Spirit

Open Heaven

Pressing In

The Thrill of Victory / The Agony of Defeat

Awed by Grace

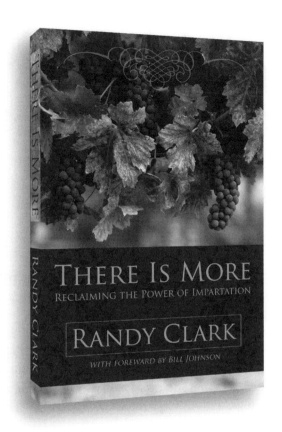

In "There Is More," Randy lays a solid biblical foundation for a theology of impartation, and takes a historical look at impartation and visitation of the Lord in the Church. This is combined with personal testimonies of people who have received an impartation throughout the world and what the impact has been in their lives. You are taken on journey throughout the world to see for yourself the lasting fruit that is taking place in the harvest field - particularly in Mozambique. This release of power is not only about phenomena of the Holy Spirit, it is about its ultimate effect on evangelism and missions. Your heart will be stirred for more as you read this book.

"This is the book that Randy Clark was born to write."

- Bill Johnson

Global School of
Supernatural
Ministry

VISION

To release followers of Christ into their specific destiny and calling, in order to live out the Great Commission.

STRUCTURE

Global School of Supernatural Ministry is a one or two year ministry school with an emphasis on impartation and equipping students for a life of walking in the supernatural. Classes start each September and end the following May. Courses are offered on-site at the Apostolic Resource Center in Mechanicsburg, PA. Upon completion of each program year a Certificate of Completion is awarded. Students seeking additional educational training may do so while attending GSSM through the Wagner Leadership Institute.

COMMUNITY

The GSSM student body is diverse in age, culture, ministry experience, and educational accomplishments. From high school graduates to professionals to retirees - the students come together seeking more of God. Supernatural power, passion and honor are key values of GSSM and are reflected in our worship, outreach and personal relationships.

For more information - or to enroll in classes - contact us at

1-866-AWAKENING or apply online at

http://gssm.globalawakening.com

globalawakening

For a schedule of upcoming events and conferences, or to purchase other products from Global Awakening, please visit our website at:

globalawakening.com